A CLOSER LOOK: GLOBAL INDUSTRIES

MEDIA AND COMMUNICATIONS INDUSTRY

ROSIE WILSON

New York

Published in 2011 by The Rosen Publishing Group Inc.
29 East 21st Street, New York, NY 10010

Editor: Susie Brooks
Consultant: Steph Warren
Designer: Rebecca Painter
Picture Researcher: Shelley Noronha

First Edition

Library of Congress Cataloging-in-Publication Data

Wilson, Rosie.
 Media and communications industry / Rosie Wilson. — 1st ed.
    p. cm. — (A closer look: global industries)
 Includes index.
 ISBN 978-1-4358-9632-1 (library binding)
 ISBN 978-1-4358-9638-3 (paperback)
 ISBN 978-1-4358-9644-4 (6-pack)
 1. Mass media—Juvenile literature. 2. Mass media and
 globalization—Juvenile literature. I. Title.
 P91.2.W539 2010
 302.23—dc22
                                    2009048162

Manufactured in Malaysia
CPSIA Compliance Information: Batch #WAS0102YA: For Further Information
Contact Rosen Publishing, New York, New York at 1-800-237-9932

Contents

CASE STUDIES
UNCOVERED

The World at Our Fingertips

Sarah walks out of school, getting out her phone and turning it on. She plugs in the headphones and listens to a track, while writing a few text messages. When she gets home, she uses her laptop to surf the web for a while, keeping her social networking site open so she can message and share links. This ad looks interesting... Eventually, she starts her homework. Sarah can't remember the exact web page shown by her teacher on the interactive whiteboard, but she quickly finds it using a search engine.

Without the global media and communications industry, Sarah's life, and many other people's lives, would be very different. Sometimes, we don't even realize how much we rely on this industry to get us through the day, because in some ways, it is invisible.

The Global Industry of Media and Communications

Global industries work across several nations and continents to create and sell their products and services. Companies working in a global industry employ and affect people in different parts of the world.

SPOTLIGHT

Globalization: a Shrinking World

Globalization means that we live in a smaller, more connected, more interdependent world. Physically, the world is not smaller, but it feels smaller because we have access to more of it. Geographical distances seem nearer because it takes less time now to travel to them or communicate between them. This has been made possible by improvements in technology. Cell phones, the internet, low-cost flights, and cheaper cars are all examples of this. Global connections are faster, easier, and cheaper, which means industries use them more. It can be easy for those living in more developed countries (MDCs) to take this for granted, but the technological revolution has not taken place at the same rate all over the world. As a result, some countries have benefited more than others from globalization.

The media and communications industry provides information, entertainment, and communication services worldwide. News media, the internet, cell phone companies, and television companies are all part of this global industry. Recently, computing has also become part of the industry, since computing is central to digital communication.

Rapid Growth

The media and communications industry has grown rapidly over the last few decades, partly due to internet use since the late 1990s. There are consumers and audiences of the industry in every country. Some products are different in every place, such as local news or advertising, and some are the same. First, new technology has allowed content (such as files, documents, and web pages) to be shared digitally and easily around the world. Second, media companies have consolidated and a small number of huge companies, often called media giants, now control most of the global market. Media is linked very closely to global trade, because without advertising and digital technology, a lot of trade would be less easy. Customers rely daily on digital technology and media companies, at work and in their personal lives.

These two middle-class Indian women, with access to digital technology and mobile communication, are typical of emerging global media markets, such as those developing in India and China.

SPOTLIGHT

Computing

Computing has played an important part in the development of the media and communications industry. In the last two decades, standardization has become popular. This means that we all use the same programs and operating systems. Microsoft produces the most popular system globally, although Apple has used the opportunities of new media (such as music downloading) to develop products and services that have attracted more customers, such as the iPod and the iPhone.

A common platform (operating system) makes it easy to share documents and files without printing. Connecting computers via networks and the internet means we can email, send reports and diagrams, and share entertainment files, such as music and videos. Businesses have saved time and money as a result. These tools would never be possible without a universal computer system, and life would be a lot slower. Even this book may become an iRead—available digitally and easily via the internet!

Economic Scale

So, how big are media companies, and how much money do they make? Although the largest companies in the world involve banking or oil, media and communications is still big business. The table below shows some of the top media and communications companies in the world, according to their success in terms of sales, profits, assets, and market value. Together, these six companies have a combined value greater than the income of Australia, the 13th-wealthiest nation in the world. If the wealthiest, General Electric, were a country, it would be the 26th-wealthiest country in the world—about the same as Greece in 2007.

This table shows some of the highest-ranking companies in the world, from *Forbes'* Global List in 2008. The list covers all industries, yet these six media and communications companies appear in the top 250.

World rank	Company	Country	Media role	What it's worth (US$ billions)
2	General Electric	U.S.A.	Holdings include NBC, History Channel	330.9
34	Telefonica	Spain	Mobile telecommunications	138.4
63	Microsoft	U.S.A.	Software and equipment (vital to media production)	253.1
119	Walt Disney	U.S.A.	ABC and ESPN news and US Weekly	61
136	News Corporation	U.S.A.	Major newspapers, news channels, and entertainment channels around the world	57.7
213	Google	U.S.A.	Leading search engine and software producer	147.7

Media Conglomerates

Over the last two decades, since the internet gained popularity, media and communications companies have gone through many mergers and takeovers. This has seen some of them grow larger and larger, so that they not only operate globally, producing a global product (such as news or music), but they also dominate the industry. Eight companies now own the major news and television channels, newspapers, web sites, and media stores worldwide, and even own many of the smaller national and regional companies (see graph below). For example, Viacom owns the television Channel CBS, the movie studio Dreamworks, the music channels MTV and VH1, Nickelodeon, and the major games web site, Shockwave. These companies operating on a larger scale can make savings through bulk buying and mass production, and have access to better financial resources. They are also able to pool resources within the company to save money. This ability to make savings as you expand is known as economy of scale.

Eight main companies now dominate the global media and communications industry, shown by the thicker lines, and own many smaller companies, some of which are shown by the smaller lines, on the chart below.

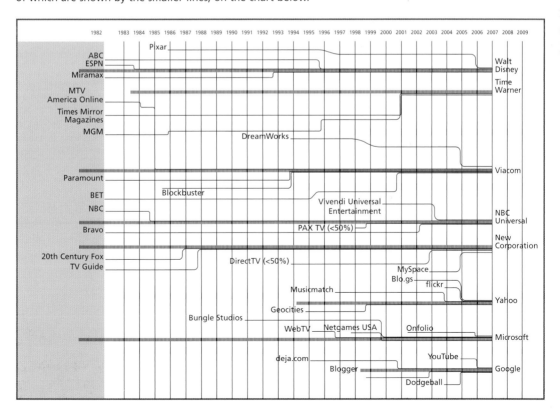

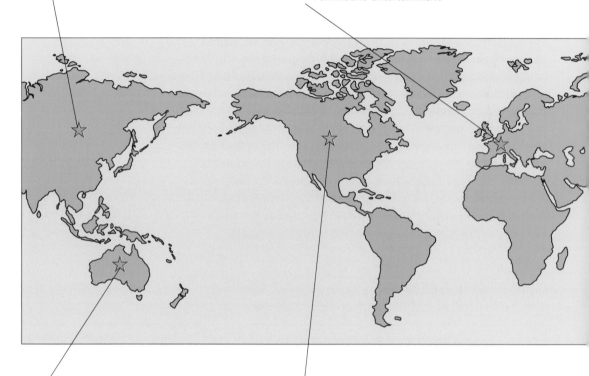

ASIA
• STAR TV Channels • TATA Sky 20% • *The Wall Street Journal Asia* • *The Far Eastern Economic Review* • HarperCollins India 40%

EUROPE
• Sky ITALIA • British Sky Broadcasting 39% (Sky News • Sky Sport, Sky 1, etc.) • *The Times* • *The Sunday Times* • *The Sun* • *News of the World* • *thelondonpaper* • *love it!* • Propertyfinder.com • HarperCollins Publishers (book publishing) • Fox Mobile Entertainment

AUSTRALIA
• Sky Network Television Limited 44%• Almost 150 newspapers and magazines, including *The Australian* • *The Weekend Australian* • *The Daily Telegraph* • *The Sunday Telegraph* • *Vogue Australia* • *GQ Australia* • HarperCollins Publishers (book publishing) • Fox Mobile Entertainment

United States
• Fox Filmed Entertainment • Fox Broadcasting Company • Fox Television Stations • *New York Post* • *The Wall Street Journal* • Fox Interactive Media (including MySpace) • HarperCollins Publishers (book publishing) • Fox Mobile Entertainment

News Corporation is one of the eight main media empires in today's global industry. Newscorp's headquarters is in New York City, and some of its holdings around the world are shown above.

Locating the Industry

Although media and communications work globally—for example, with news stations in every major city—the largest and most powerful companies are in the West. This usually means the United States and Europe. Most media products reflect a Western consumer's way of life. For this reason, a CNN or BBC reporter who is from the United States or the UK will report news from around the world in a way that is relevant to our lives. For instance, the headlines in the U.S. and UK newspapers about the hotel bombings in Mumbai in November 2008 prioritized news about the Westerners involved. In the same way, entertainment such as music we listen to, is mainly from Europe and the U.S.A., even though we have access to culture from around the world.

Who Benefits?

Globalization has so far benefited certain Western countries more than the rest of the world. The global media industry demonstrates this, since it is based mainly in the U.S.A. and Europe. The main companies are registered in these regions, and the profits from movies, TV, and other media products bought globally find their way back to these countries.

Interestingly, an exception is in communications—the cell phone is very popular even in the poorest countries. Cell phone technology is available in most of urban Africa, for example, and has enabled South African communications companies to grow. It has even improved literacy rates, since sending a written text message is cheaper than calling. As growing economies join the global market, especially India, China, South Korea, Brazil, and Russia, they will impact on the global media and communications industry. There will be more demand for stories and products concerning these nations, and new media empires may emerge.

> *...in the emerging world, we are seeing the creation of a global middle class of more than two billion people...and as they advance, they will be increasingly hungry for better sources of news and entertainment.*

Rupert Murdoch, News Corporation AGM, 2008

SPOTLIGHT

The Digital Divide

The "digital divide" describes a divide between people who can access digital media and communications, such as broadband internet and digital television, and people who cannot. Sometimes, these groups are called the "information rich" and the "information poor." This divide is global, because some world regions simply do not have access to the internet.

The divide is also a social divide within each nation, between those with digital access and skills and those without. This divide is becoming a new measure of global and local inequality. Mostly, people who frequently use a variety of digital media are young, and in the West.

The media and communications industry affects almost everything we do. Many industries rely on communications technology, such as email, to be able to do their business. Our personal lives are also dependent on media technology. But this relationship between industry and consumer is interdependent—the media and communications industry needs us in order to survive. If we stopped buying newspapers, using our phones, watching television, and turning on our computers, the industry would lose its customers and its profit.

Global Exchange

The power of the media can affect whole countries. News stories have affected tourism industries and national economies. For instance, in China and Hong Kong, tourism declined when the SARS epidemic in Asia hit the global news in 2002. Nations also respond to each other's national media, as in the example of the British *Big Brother* program in which Shilpa Shetty, an Indian Bollywood actress, took part. When there was a scandal surrounding the 2007 program, the global media coverage created a reaction in India, her home country, as well as in the UK. This led to a UK contestant, Jade Goody, appearing on *Bigg Boss*, the Indian version of *Big Brother*, as the only non-Indian, in an effort to restore her reputation with Indian people.

> *[The internet] allows people to do what they want to do more efficiently. It allows people to exist in an information space which doesn't know geographical boundaries. My hope is that it'll be very positive in bringing people together around the planet, because it'll make communication between different countries more possible...*
>
> Tim Berners Lee, the inventor of the internet, 2005

Citizens of the Media World

It is now possible for almost anyone to become part of the media. Members of the public send in their images and video footage of events to news and entertainment web sites and channels. They give their opinions, too, through blogs, text messages, and emails. People check online reviews by customers before they buy a product such as a television, rather than simply using ads. Computer software that has been developed by the public is also appearing. People are mostly not paid for this citizen media. On the whole, we still rely on the large media companies to provide information, entertainment, and methods of communication.

SPOTLIGHT

More Choice?

Global media and communications make us globally connected and we have more choice in entertainment, news, music, and personal communications. There are different news perspectives, different ways to experience and interact with media, and faster and broader coverage of the world. But many people argue that the way global media works actually limits our choice, because so many media products come from the same companies. This means that in some ways, not everyone around the world has equal access to the media or equal freedom to express their views. Cultural diversity is affected by globalization—as Western culture spreads, some cultures do not have a voice if there is no media giant backing them.

A customer in India reads a headline about the star Shilpa Shetty, in the British reality TV show *Big Brother*. Global media coverage of national events can create strong reactions in other countries, and can even impact on relationships between governments.

Using the Media

Many organizations use the media to make change happen. They publish a story that will influence the behavior of both companies and individuals. For example, the Corpwatch web site published an article in 2004 about working conditions in a Chinese factory making toys for Walmart. The article, which came from the Reuters news agency, said that the laws regarding legal pay and maximum hours were not being met. As a result of this, some people chose to boycott Walmart. In 2008, after a series of similar news reports criticizing the company, Walmart has announced a new ethical and sustainability policy to monitor the factories that it uses.

Promoting People

The 2008 Presidential election in the United States showed how the global media industry can be used to organize people and to persuade people to vote in a particular way. Television, news, and advertising media have always played an important role in politics, but Barack Obama's team used all the digital media available to promote their presidential candidate. They created an account for him on the social networking site Facebook, and on other popular sites, which has engaged millions of supporters.

Political Networking

Obama's own web site, my.barackobama.com, was developed with one of the founders of Facebook. The campaign team used the site to collect donations, keep people informed with regular updates, and let supporters organize local events. Volunteers communicated, and perhaps most importantly, the site engaged young voters— Obama won two-thirds of voters ages 18–29. Another part of the industry used was mobile communication. Supporters signed up to receive a text message update about the campaign, and the phone numbers collected were saved and used to call voters around election day, to persuade or remind people to vote. Since Barack Obama won the election, his social-networking success has been studied by groups wanting similar results.

Outsourcing

Some media companies have their sales teams in one country, but their customer support is outsourced to less developed countries (LDCs). This has positive impacts for the LDCs, such as

creating new jobs and new economic centers, such as
Bangalore in south India. There is an increase in training and
also positive effects in education, and the country's national
economy improves. However, there has been anger in
countries that have lost jobs to LDCs, and people complain
that because of cultural differences and geographical distance,
these global call centers cannot provide a good service.

Global Connections

As the media and communications industry has globalized,
it has impacted on communities and environments around
the world. Many companies manufacture consumer
electronics in Asia, then fly the products around the world
to be sold in retail outlets or stored in a warehouse and
sold over the internet. Workers who manage these processes
need to visit the countries involved, so they fly, too. All air
travel emits carbon dioxide and other greenhouse gases into
the atmosphere, therefore, the global media industry and
other global trade connections are criticized for contributing
to climate change. Health issues have arisen, too, and some
people fear that wireless networks for broadband internet
and cell phone masts may have serious effects, such as
causing cancer.

MySpace and MTV
present a dialogue
with Barack
Obama. During his
election campaign,
Obama engaged
with young people
through new
media, such as
social networking
and text messages,
in order to gather
support.

Environmental Impacts

Media production can also affect people and the environment through filming. A movie called *The Beach* was released in 2000, based on a beautiful, isolated island in Thailand where a global community lived. The filming itself had an impact on the island, because plants were cleared and sand washed away. Tourism to that part of the world also increased, so that the calm "paradise" that the movie was about disappeared. More recently, in 2007, the director of *Batman: The Dark Knight*, Christopher Nolan, asked the residents and businesses of Hong Kong to leave their lights on during nighttime filming to illuminate the city. The citizens mostly ignored the request, and Nolan was criticized for not thinking of the environment.

Out with the Old...

The fashion for new phones, faster computers, and better-quality products is creating large amounts of electronic waste. As technology moves on, new replacements, such as blu-ray and nanoPods, make people throw away old devices. Sometimes the gadgets are deliberately produced with a short lifespan, so that we will buy a newer device and spend money again. This is called planned obsolescence. The richest countries that consume the fastest create the most waste, which is often exported to poorer countries for processing. This hides the problem and means that some workers in LDCs have highly dangerous jobs, and are exposed to harmful substances such as lead and arsenic. For instance, Lagos in Nigeria receives 100,000 waste computers a month, and many of these are burned, releasing toxic fumes and causing barium and mercury to be leached into the soil.

SPOTLIGHT

Greenwash

Greenwash is a name used when something is advertized as "green," in order to sell it or attract people to it, but the product is not as "green" as it appears. For example, it could be made from sustainable materials, but shipped a long way, which still emits carbon into the atmosphere. Ads about "green" issues bombard us in all media, and companies use "green" or environmental messages to sell their products through the media and communications industry, too. Banks, car manufacturers, and energy providers all use advertising to make themselves look like sustainable companies, and many of these groups often also tell customers what to do in order to look after the environment. Perhaps telling us that they are "good" makes us buy more, but green marketing and greenwash are really sales tactics like any others—they are just less obvious.

The global media industry relies on regular updates, which results in large amounts of electronic waste being produced. The old products that people and businesses discard end up in piles of digital garbage, such as this one in China, as they are replaced with new hardware that includes the latest technology.

One Global Culture

Media products are part of our culture, so in some ways, the world is developing a global, universal culture, even sometimes called "the global brain." Movies, bands, and television programs are aired all around the world, and our access to news and information is universal. Media products help us to understand other places, too, so global culture becomes "multicultural." For example, we can listen to music from Latin America, and learn about aspects of other cultures through credit card commercials. We can even see news footage of places where the governments have forbidden foreigners to visit, such as Myanmar (Burma). News channels published cell phone video footage from inside Myanmar during riots in September 2007.

Shouting the Loudest

The media and communications industry does not incorporate all cultures, though, and the "global culture" is more representative of a wealthy, Western elite within the global population. Since the largest companies are mainly from the United States, the English language dominates the media, and Western values do, too. For example, U.S. programs such as *Heroes*, *Battlestar Galactica*, and *Friends* are exported globally. However, U.S. imports, including the British program *The Office* and the Australian program *Kath & Kim*, were made more "culturally appropriate" in versions of the sitcoms filmed in Los Angeles, using American actors. This means that although some foreigners might learn about American culture through television, Americans are less likely to experience other cultures by watching imports. Television imported from Africa or Asia is rare, which limits our cultural knowledge further.

Diverse Media Communities

New media has brought more examples of cultural diversity, especially where smaller companies and citizen media are concerned. Because technology is cheap and most people have access to the internet, web sites such as YouTube and MySpace allow people from different cultures to create popular media products, such as funny videos or recordings of music performances. This is also a way for communities around the world to communicate, and live the cultural lifestyle they want, for instance, by importing food, clothes, and music from another country.

One Media Device

The future of the media and communications industry could involve more standardization, and creating a common platform so that we can get all our media products and services in one place. Television, the internet, music, and news all coming from one single device could make media much more convenient. This has been trialed by some companies already, and is being developed, so the next few years may bring all available media, especially entertainment, to those who can afford it—the "information rich."

Our Media Future

We have more ways than ever before to have fun, communicate, and even to waste time—but only some of us can do this. Many people in the world are without the basic requirements of food, water, and shelter, and some do not have the freedom to express their opinions without being arrested or killed. The "luxury" of multimedia is unimaginable to them. Many of us are obsessed with buying the fastest, shiniest, and cleverest gadgets, and a news story about the release of a new gadget often pushes out a news story about poverty elsewhere in the world. The challenge will be how we use the ever-newer media available to us, and also how we make sure it is available to everyone.

Passersby in Kochi, Uganda, look at ads, including the Celltel cell phone campaign using the slogan "Join our world." People who do not have access to computers and cell phones are increasingly left out of the "global world."

The news and information industry is central to global media, and this subindustry is often described as simply "the media" ("new media" usually refers to anything available online). News and information products and services overlap into many areas of media, including advertising and personal communication. The industry has adapted to the development of digital technology over the last two decades.

Journalists format the news in video, audio, and written headlines, often managing live feeds of reportage as events happen. France 24 is an international, round-the-clock news channel based in Paris, France.

Digital Media

The internet has become faster, bigger, and more reliable, and it has been used to share news and information. A story that breaks in Japan can be known about seconds later in the U.S.A., and within the hour, images, video, and audio can be sent to U.S. media headquarters using the internet and shared with the public through television. As the world has globalized, audiences want more global content, made possible through technological developments.

Commercial Industry

News media have diversified, and you can consume news stories or facts in different ways. The introduction of multiplatform media (television, interactive, online, and so on) changed a public service into a commercial industry. Media giants own companies across different formats, so they can take a news story and package it for TV, radio, the internet, and newspapers. This makes news cheaper to broadcast and means that a multiformat story makes more profit. Because of this, corporations tend to prioritize news stories that work across formats or platforms, and so can be sold to TV and radio networks, newspapers, and magazines, and increasingly, to internet service providers. In turn, these media platforms earn money to purchase news stories through advertising or license fees and in some cases, government funding.

A news story is processed in many different formats. The process, shown below, often involves several employees in a news company (such as the one pictured on page 20).

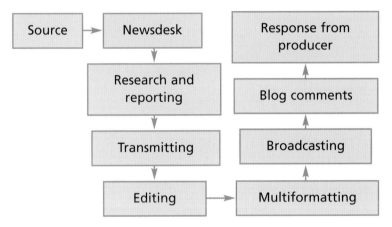

PERSPECTIVES FOR DEBATE

"Media conglomerates exist simply to make money by selling light escapist entertainment."

Robert W. McChesney in *Who Owns the Global Media?*, 2004

"The media are generally meant to contribute to the strengthening of peace, international understanding, and fighting racism, apartheid, and incitement to war."

Dr. Mostafa Masmoudi, Professor of Communication Policies, 2008

SPOTLIGHT

Online Information

Two ways we get information online are through blogs (web logs) and web sites such as Wikipedia, which is created by its users. Blogs are mainly amateur and free, created by people who want to write online, rather than for a corporation. Anyone can contribute information to Wikipedia, which is then checked by staff. Wikipedia is a nonprofit organization that claims to be the fourth-most-visited web site in the world and states that it is built on values of common sharing of the "sum of all knowledge" through the internet. Although these models came first, media corporations are now producing their own blogs and wikis. There are blogs written by news reporters for the major networks, and *Encyclopedia Britannica* constantly updates its web site, to compete as a popular information site.

Fact or Fiction?

Dramatic style, such as catchy headlines, eye-catching graphics, and shocking images, sells more newspapers and attracts more viewers, so the presentation of information in the media has also changed in recent years. Sometimes owners of media empires decide what the world "should" know, based on their political viewpoints. Silvio Berlusconi, who has been elected Prime Minister of Italy three times, was criticized during election campaigns because it was said that the three main television networks, which he controls, represented him too positively. Rupert Murdoch, owner of the News Corp empire, is known for his political right-wing views, and other media companies suggest that he has too much control over the content of the world press.

> *Rupert Murdoch argued strongly for a war with Iraq in an interview this week. Which might explain why his 175 editors around the world are backing it, too.*
>
> The Guardian, 2003

Controlling the News

A handful of companies control the news market, which is called an oligopoly. Many of these businesses also own entertainment production companies, and people argue that the line between information and entertainment has blurred: infotainment has appeared. News channels often review television shows and products made by the same company. For example, the UK's BBC regularly reviews BBC products on its morning news program, and ABC News recently featured a sock puppet on *Good Morning America* from Pets.com. The parent company of ABC Disney owned 5 percent of Pets.com, so many said that the news program had actually advertised Pets.com for its own gain.

Global Impacts

The globalization of the news and information industry lets us have instant access to information around the world. Global media reporting can affect the global economy, too, such as during the financial crisis in 2008. An example of this is when the British media reported that the bank, Northern Rock, was in trouble, then began reporting the long lines outside banks where panicked savers were withdrawing their money. The news coverage continued daily, until so many people withdrew their money that the bank collapsed, for which some blame the media. Continuous news coverage and immediate internet broadcasting all over the world arguably did put banks in more trouble. This then gave more bad news to be reported, and the cycle continued.

> *I don't think there is a future for large numbers of [TV] news channels in Britain. It's moving so fast to the web, and their numbers—all the news channels—are so pitifully small. Increasingly, if there's a major news development, you are going to the web first to find out what's happening.*
>
> Jon Snow, BBC journalist, 2006

Global Pirates

Another example of a global story is the report of the oil tanker seized by Somali pirates in November 2008. The event was reported daily all over the world as it unfolded. This was because ships from many different nations had been seized, but also because the trade route through the Suez Canal is important for many wealthy nations. The tanker was carrying oil worth $100 million, which was relevant to everyone interested in the increasing price of oil. Oil-producing nations such as Nigeria also followed the story closely, since it affected their oil markets. Other global events affected more people, such as the civil war in the Democratic Republic of Congo, but they were not as popular at the time.

The Liberian oil tanker, *MV Sirius Star*, was hijacked by Somali pirates off the coast of Kenya in November 2008. Globally, many news web sites and channels reported news concerning this event, which caused the price of oil to jump by more than $1 a barrel around the world.

Information Literacy

Understanding how the media works is important when it plays such a big part in our lives. "Media literacy" has recently been studied in schools across the world. It includes understanding how the media makes money, and how that influences what we see, hear, and experience. But how do we know what our connection to the global media and communications industry is? Some useful questions might be:

• How often do I use media products?
• How do I choose my media product?
• What culture does my product come from?
• How does it make money?
• How factual is it?
• What do I think about when I create my own media products (for example, profiles or blogs online)?

As well as media literacy, information literacy and cultural literacy are also discussed as skills that are important to help us interact with the global media industry. These skills help us to identify the values of each company, and think about who their intended audience is.

Freedom of Choice

Can we do anything about the media influencing our lives? As consumers we have choices, such as the newspaper we buy, the TV we watch, the web pages we browse. However, our choices may not always be as free as we think. Sometimes nations put very strict controls on the media, such as in China, where certain search terms on Google and Yahoo! are blocked, stopping access to web sites. The terms include "democracy China," "Tibet," and "equality." Western nations, too, may begin to monitor internet browsing habits for national security. If this happens, someone could legally read everything you type online!

Google.cn, the Chinese version of the popular internet search engine, has censored its users' searches, in agreement with the Chinese government. Although internet freedoms improved briefly during the Beijing Olympics in 2008, today, China monitors and restricts many public opinion web sites.

> *Media literacy [is] understanding how the media function, how they construct reality and create meaning, and how they are organized as well as knowing how to use the media in a sensible way.*

Ullah Carlson, UNESCO report, 2006

SPOTLIGHT

Media Influence and Regulation

There are a number of different organizations that influence the news media. Some are national, such as the Federal Communications Commision (FCC) in the U.S.A., Ofcom in the UK, and the Australian Communications and Media Authority (ACMA). These set out regulations and guidelines for standards of broadcasting within their countries. There are also global bodies, such as UNESCO and the World Trade Organization (WTO), that influence the quality, neutrality, and even the "safety" of the global media industry. UNESCO supports independent media showing different perspectives.

Digitalization of the media industry has allowed us to have access to news instantly. This news screen at Canary Wharf in London, UK, showed the latest available information about attempted terrorist attacks on the Underground in July 2005. Many Londoners used cell phones to contact their family.

Advertising: Tempting the World to Buy

The advertising industry has been global ever since the 1950s, when global communications and transportation began to get cheaper and easier. Manufacturers therefore looked for new markets to expand into, and advertising became a central part of this. The growth at this time was helped by an increase in the number of families owning televisions. Today, similar advertising techniques are used across many MDCs. Increasingly, we share the same products and brand names globally, too. Ads and commercials give reasons why the consumer should buy certain products and persuade us using images and catchy language. Whereas traditional, small-scale advertising featured one person or image, this has been replaced with stylish, dramatic, and multimedia campaigns that often have large budgets.

Today's advertising companies might use television, radio, and the internet to promote a product, as well as newspapers and magazines. More recently, pre-recorded phone messages and text messages to cell phones have been introduced. In LDCs, advertising is also present, but cheaper techniques may be used, such as word of mouth, billboards, and painting on buildings.

Ads are part of the urban landscape in cities across the world, such as New York, below. Do these ads influence us or do we ignore them?

Advertising Regulation

Digital media has allowed many companies to advertise their products through a web site, which people find by browsing. Although older media such as television and newspapers have advertising standards or rules, in most MDCs, regulation of the internet is very new. Ads are sometimes misleading or do not make clear that their purpose is advertising. Consumers have bought products online that do not exist, or do not work, such as designer handbags that prove to be fake. One man thought he had bought a DVD player, but then only received a discount voucher. Even television standards vary. For instance, commercials for Maggi Noodles from Bangladesh that were accidentally broadcast in the UK broke the rules of the Advertising Standards Authority (ASA). The claims that Horlicks made children "taller, stronger, and sharper," and that Maggi helps to "build strong muscles and bones" did not meet standards for truth in advertising in the UK, but were regularly broadcast legally in Bangladesh.

Global Brands

Brands are central to the retail industry, and many companies, especially global transnational companies (TNCs), use advertising to develop their brand. A brand can be a mark or trademark, such as a logo, but it has also been described as the "personality" of a product—and brands can be created through advertising. We are all familiar with global brands such as McDonalds, Coke, Nike, Toyota, and so on. People believe that brands show quality or make the consumer fashionable, so they buy things that show a mark that they recognize and convey what they want to say about themselves.

Sounding Out the Brand

TNCs with popular, successful brands can be more flexible in commercials—sometimes reminding audiences about the brand or trademark is enough, rather than giving more reasons to buy as well. The "I'm lovin' it" campaign for McDonalds created a new dimension to their already popular brand: sound. The five-note tune that played on their television and movie theater ads stuck in customers' heads, reminding them of the company and its products. McDonalds, who have a large budget so they can experiment with media, are also using podcasts, and even introducing a music-sharing station in-store in Chicago.

Imagining the World

As ads become more imaginative, they arguably help us to understand more about the global world in which we live. Car ads show panoramic landscapes from around the world, and one HSBC Bank advertising campaign used the idea of culture shock and different cultures to promote itself as a global bank, with the motto "Never underestimate the importance of local knowledge." However, ads don't portray the whole picture, because they are limited by their goal—to make people consume. This means that wealthy economies and people with disposable income will be targeted, and represented more in advertising.

Giant Campaigns

A recent high-budget, multiplatform advertising campaign was centered on the James Bond movie, *Quantum of Solace*. James Bond and 007 are successful brands—people understand what the brand will deliver, and many consumers buy into it. The media production company, Time Warner, had its own web advertising (including downloads such as screensavers) and used trailers in theaters and a theme song with the band, The Raconteurs, as well as publicity including interviews with the stars. But Time Warner also worked with other companies who had their own products to advertise. Customers then associate the brand of James Bond (smart, stylish, dramatic) with the other products, such as Coca-Cola's Coke Zero drink, which rebranded as Coke ZeroZero7. Even large organizations such as visitBritain and the British military Royal Marines recruitment campaign included James Bond in their advertising while the movie was being promoted.

The Swiss watchmaker, Omega, produced a limited edition watch for *Quantum of Solace*. James Bond actor Daniel Craig wears the watch in the movie.

The Buzz for Brands Associated with James Bond

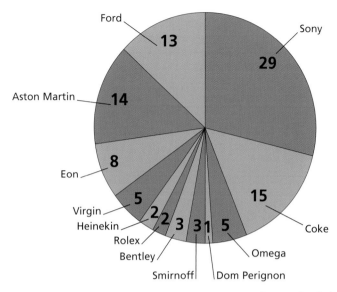

Source: Onalytica

This graph shows how much "buzz" each brand associated with Bond has created on the web. People's conversations about *Quantum of Solace*, James Bond, and the brands above were measured, to find out which brands were most popular, and which ads were most successful.

Advertising and Health

Global advertising is sometimes criticized for encouraging us to do unhealthy things. Some people believe that advertising of fast food and computer games has led to a growing problem of childhood obesity. In 2004, a global report stated that 1 in 10 children were overweight—a total of 155 million worldwide. The World Health Organization (WHO) recommended that advertising should promote healthy eating, and banning the advertising of fast food during children's programs is also being discussed.

SPOTLIGHT

Advertising for Good?
Governments, charities, and other organisations also use advertising. Some ads ask for money, such as those by Oxfam, Cancer Research, or Islamic Relief. Others attempt to change our behavior, perhaps by persuading people to recycle or to sign a petition. Even businesses have begun using ads to change behavior, especially due to the increased interest in environmental issues. Energy companies tell us to turn down our central heating, clothing labels tell us to wash at lower temperatures, and manufacturers advertise how "green" or "environmentally friendly" items are, giving us another reason to buy them.

Car advertising, such as this billboard in China, can increase our global understanding, as we are shown landscapes from around the world.

How Many Ads?

The average American encounters between 600 and 625 ads a day, but may not notice them all. In most MDCs, the figure may be the same, and will vary depending on lifestyle. In the United States, 272 of those ads are through television, radio, newspapers, and magazines, leaving the rest to the internet, environment (billboards, plasma screens, etc.), and possibly telesales. So what does this mean for readers of this book? How, when, and where do you encounter ads? Are the ads successful? Most importantly, are you always aware that a product is being advertised?

> *Television and advertising are simply cultivated addictions, designed to control people in a particular way.*
>
> Noam Chomsky, Corpwatch, 1996

Transparency and Literacy

A major issue with modern advertising is its lack of transparency—it is not always clear when we are being persuaded to buy something. Large budgets mean that advertisers can use many different formats, and make highly produced, imaginative ads that influence us by entertainment. In order to choose carefully, we have to be critical of what we see.

When Advertisers Use Personal Data

Personal data is gathered through market research, surveys, and companies selling information such as addresses. Recently, technology has provided new ways for companies to collect data on our interests and the things that we buy. For example, supermarkets use bonus point schemes to scan our shopping and learn what items we choose. Then ads and promotions are sent to us to match our tastes. Another way of using personal data is by sharing general customer data. Amazon.com does this by offering "frequently bought together" and "customers who bought this also bought" sections, to generate more sales. Google uses cookies to save all searches that you do, for up to 30 years, and AOL (America Online) published such data for over 500,000 of its users. There were many criticisms of this, and some users were identified by the media. AOL apologized to all concerned, and said that the release of the data had been a mistake, but that it does still collect search data. User-generated content is also collected from blogs and web sites visited, and it is used for companies to understand their market. The main issue is when consumers are unaware of how their data helps advertising companies to target them.

Staff at online media company Amazon.com's UK distribution center prepare to send out 65,000 copies of *Harry Potter and the Goblet of Fire*. The company used its own web site to generate hype, advertise the release date of the book, and take pre-orders.

The Music Industry: Going Digital

Consumerism has gradually changed music from cultural expression or ritual into a global industry where songs are bought and sold. Artists, record companies, and music stores all profit through sales, but the way that profits are made is changing fast, now that digital technology formats music as a data file. The merging of media businesses has included record companies, and there are now four major music companies: EMI, Sony BMG, Universal, and Warner. These record companies, or labels, produce and sell artists' music, but their future is unclear now that CDs are not as popular as digital files.

Music Industry Product Flow Chart

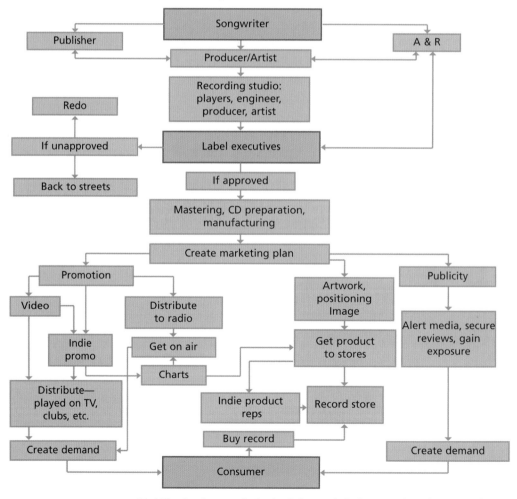

Digitilization has revolutionized the music industry. Before sharing and downloading, artists relied on a complex production and marketing process to release their music, as set out in this flow chart.

The Social Role of Music

Music has a long history of global connections. The Atlantic Slave Trade took African working music to the Americas, which then became jazz, and Irish music has spread around the world with the movement of Irish people. In this way, music is cultural expression, and sometimes it is used for political messages, too, bringing musicians and fans together for a message, such as HIV/AIDS awareness. Amnesty International sells music and other cultural products online, perhaps to connect humans around the world, as part of their campaign. Organizations are also finding new ways of using music for political reasons. One example is Calabash, a fair trade music company that sells online music and allows fans to fund small, lesser-known musicians from around the world through sales and sponsorship, instead of the bulk of the money for music going to the record company.

Piracy

Record labels and record stores have lost money in the last few years, since people now share music, which reduces sales, and people also download music from the internet, sometimes for free and sometimes paying. Because digital music is easy to download, copy, and share, there has been a global debate about music piracy. In 2008, a UK survey found that the average young person had 800 illegal music tracks on their mp3 player. One artist, Prince, tried unsuccessfully to stop his music being downloaded without copyright, by filing a lawsuit against the web site that hosted the tracks.

PERSPECTIVES FOR DEBATE

"If you're getting music for free that you'd usually have to pay for, you're committing a crime."

Directgov web site, 2008

"Yeah, I love it. I think it's brilliant ...Music should be shared."

Joss Stone, musician, 2008

SPOTLIGHT

Global Piracy

- Nearly 20 billion songs were swapped or downloaded illegally in 2005.
- The cost of sound recording piracy to the U.S. economy in 2007 was $3.7 billion dollars.
- In Mexico, music sales dropped by 25 percent in 2007 as illegal downloading became more popular.

Technology

The music industry has experienced positive and negative impacts of the new technologies available. Tracks can now be sent easily, but to do this, most files have been compressed, which makes them smaller and in most cases, leaves out some of the detailed data. The most popular format, the MPEG Layer 3 or mp3, uses this technique, and some listeners complain that the quality is not as good as on CDs or vinyl records.

Members of the public try new products, including the iPod nano, in an Apple store in London. The design, style, and color of media products influences buyers, since gadgets are also considered fashion items.

Where's the Money?

Since music sharing began, there has been a fall in CD sales, and even sites where music is bought digitally are not making a great amount of profit. In this changing industry, some of the ways that companies and artists are working, or plan to work in the future, are:

- increasing the prices of live concerts for fans, to raise profit;
- selling directly through stylish, up-to-date artists' web sites;
- providing other sale items such as merchandise, limited edition albums, etc.;
- asking for companies that profit from music content, such as broadband suppliers and phone networks, to pay a "music tax";
- providing a web site where all music is free to members who pay a monthly subscription fee, as Napster does;
- providing free music for listeners, with an ad at the

beginning of the music track (the advertiser pays for the time), as QTrax does;
• building a fanbase through web sites such as MySpace, Youtube, and Facebook before releasing an album for sale.

Companies that sell new media music products and services, such as Napster and MSN Music store, expect that they will make money in the future. iTunes is an example of a company that is already profiting, and it currently holds 70 percent of the digital music market.

I think this is an exciting time to be an artist. On the one hand, the internet has destroyed the old music business, but what is beginning to be created is a lot more exciting.

Peter Gabriel, music artist and producer, 2008

Impact on the Environment

Digital music reduces the materials we use, such as CD cases and bags, but the mp3 players and computers that we play music on are updated regularly, which creates large amounts of electronic waste. Musicians have an impact on the world environment—they go on global tours, which involve people flying and driving to venues. These concerts produce waste such as food and beverage packaging. However, some musicians are aware of their impact on the environment and use their fame to raise awareness about environmental issues, through concerts, blogs, and interviews.

SPOTLIGHT

Radiohead

In Rainbows, the band Radiohead's 2007 album, was an experiment in music downloading. The band (they didn't have a record label) made the album available for fans to pay "as much as they thought it was worth," which ended up being an average of $5.50. The experiment showed that the music industry is radically changing. It is difficult to tell how money will be made in the future. Radiohead also used the internet to decide where to run their gigs based on the overall carbon footprint of different locations, which included how much travel would be involved for the band and fans to get to the venues. They are arguably in the luxurious position of being rich enough to think about the environment and take risks, because they became successful through being supported by a record label originally. Many musicians are less able to control the new music industry.

Personal Communication: in a Shrinking World

The global media and communications industry has changed the way we keep in touch. Letters sent through the mail are unpopular now, and are nicknamed "snail mail" because email, instant messaging, and cell phones make it easy to communicate quickly wherever we are. Phone calls from landline to landline have also become less popular. As communications technology has globalized and diversified, it has enabled us to be more flexible in our personal lives. We can contact people more often and when we want, so arrangements and friendships are easier to make.

Web 2.0

The internet is only in its second decade of worldwide use, but the way people use it and make money from it is changing. Web 2.0 is an idea that has been around since 2004, and it describes the new ways people use the internet, such as chatting and social networking online. People communicate and share content such as links, images, and videos on the web. The social networking site Facebook is used by more than 120 million people worldwide, although Myspace is still more popular in the United States. These sites allow you to create your own page, contact friends by message, chat to them, and share content. They also have games and quizzes, so personal communication is being mixed with entertainment.

Too Personal?

As the web has become a social place, some people are now concerned that others have too much access to their personal details. For example, when users send or receive anything using Google's email service, Gmail, the software selects ads based on the content of the messages and displays relevant ads immediately. Worryingly for many students in the United States, college staff viewed Facebook and MySpace profiles to help them decide whether or not to accept candidates' applications.

Although data protection laws prohibit some data being sold, kept, or used for something we were not aware of, there are no data protection laws governing our user-generated content online. Since our personal communication depends on the global media industry, we are bombarded with even more ads. Evidence suggests that most people don't click on ads while they are in a "social" mood, but only when they are actively searching for something.

Flexible Phones

High-speed internet access is currently impossible for many, because of prices, unreliable power supply, and living in remote areas. However, the cell phone is a new media product that has flourished globally; around 28 percent of Africans now have a cell phone, for example. The cell phone uses only a small amount of power, and because of its battery, it is not affected by the power cuts that are frequent in some African countries. Worldwide, cell phone technology allows flexibility, so people can make arrangements spontaneously, and they can even use the internet and email through their phones.

This social networking site allows global interaction with friends, and the sharing of events and information. Although Facebook's site claims that "Anyone can join," the digital divide means that many people do not have access to this media.

Smaller World

Living, working, and traveling globally is made easier by the media and communications industry. People feel that they are always connected to their friends and family, because they can email, text message them, and send photographs. Voice over internet protocol (VOIP) has made international calling even cheaper, and Skype, the most popular VOIP company, has 220 million users across the world.

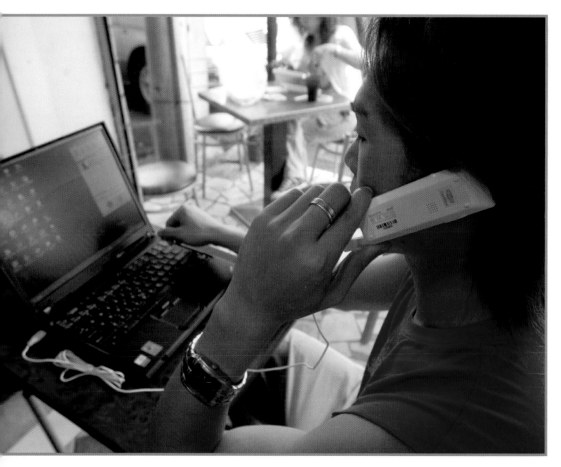

A man uses a Skype internet phone next to a laptop in Taipei. Taiwanese telephone handset makers have capitalized on the extraordinary success of Skype, offering users plug-in phones for their computers and other Skype-compatible devices.

Media companies make traveling easier, too. The backpacker online community web sites, travelgeneration.com and lonelyplanet.tv, are both media ventures that encourage travelers to create and interact with multimedia products, including video, images, blogs, and links to other travel company sites. This allows travelers to share advice and reviews of places they have visited. Flickr is a web site to which people can upload their images to share with family and friends, directly from their cell phones. These products and services use the opportunity of global travel and migration to create a new kind of media product.

Media Danger

Easier personal communication has also created a potentially unsafe environment, especially for young people and children. There is a lot of adult content on the internet, and it is difficult to protect children from it. One example of this is anorexia web sites. Many young people suffer from anorexia, and Bebo, Facebook, YouTube, Yahoo!, and MySpace have all been criticized for allowing groups and pages that encourage sufferers to starve, exchange tips, and keep up "motivation." Yahoo! removed 115 anorexia web sites in 2001. Other serious issues such as child abuse are discussed widely. The United Nations (UN) recently published a report saying that children and young people need to be protected from, but also prepared for, harmful content online.

> *There is no quality control on the internet.*
>
> Kai Hafez, *The Myth of Media Globalization*, 2007

A government-funded billboard in Nigeria warns against internet scams, classified as crime 419. Nigerian scams are globally famous, and many Westerners have been duped into giving money through an email that they have received.

PERSPECTIVES FOR DEBATE

"User-generated content is a new market research tool, and a new way to build a closer relationship with your target market."

BrandRepublic.com, 2006

"It's mine—you can't have it. If you want to use it for something, then you have to negotiate with me. I have to agree, I have to understand what I'm getting in return."

Tim Berners-Lee, on his own user-generated content, collected by companies online, 2008

SPOTLIGHT

Cell Phones: War and Waste

War

Industry experts predicted that 1.26 billion cell phones would be sold in 2008, and many of these contain the mineral columbite tantalite (coltan) from mines in the Democratic Republic of Congo. There is a civil war in the region, and the minerals fuel this war because many mines are held by rebel fighters. The money made is used to buy arms and bribes that result in the deaths and displacement of hundreds of thousands of civilians. Coltan deposits are present in other countries, too, but have not yet been used—perhaps because mines ruin the landscape and mining work is tough and low-paid.

Waste

Most phone handsets are replaced after 18 months, and the waste (which is often toxic or hazardous), is exported to poorer countries to process. Companies have created new ways to get rid of a phone, by selling it onward, by recycling it, or by turning it into a personal alarm for women. One organization sends phones to U.S. soldiers away from home, allowing them to call their families.

Spanish civil guardsmen carry a computer confiscated from the office of the terrorist group ETA's political wing. The monitoring of media interaction can sometimes be used as evidence, and can aid detection of crimes.

The Product and the Audience

In 2006, *Time* magazine's Person of the Year was announced as "You"—the public—because of the way that Web 2.0 has enabled "us" to get involved in media and communications. Letters to the editor and phone-ins have been replaced with text messages, emails, videos, and blogs, and they are much more common. Everyone who has access to the internet or a cell phone has an opportunity to voice opinions about issues, and media companies are responding to this wave, since they have to give audiences what they want in order to make money. Citizen media (also called commons media) and web communities are having a real impact on people's decisions about what they buy and where they go.

Social networking sites and other personal communication media present new opportunities for business. The musician and TV presenter, Lily Allen, created a large fan base via word-of-mouth on MySpace, and uploaded some tracks for free, then used her record label and a multiformat campaign to successfully launch her album.

Becoming an Active Global Citizen

What is an active global citizen? It is someone who tries, in their own small way, to make the world a better place. To become an active global citizen, you will need to get involved in decisions that others make about your life and the lives of others around the world. Consider how the world could be changed, such as improving the environment and political or social conditions for others, and seek information about the issues from a wide variety of sources. Then go public by presenting your arguments to others, from classmates and local groups, to national politicians and global organizations.

In Your Life

Sometimes, we don't realize that we are all connected to the global media and communications industry every day. Another thing that we often forget is that all media we interact with—phones, TV programs, etc., have been made by a company to sell to consumers, either directly or indirectly. A study published the below figures for the interaction of the average young person (ages 14–24) with various media.

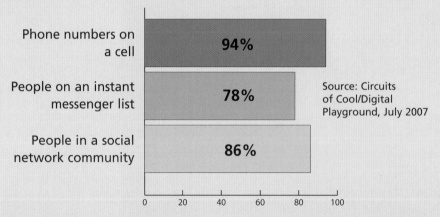

Phone numbers on a cell: **94%**

People on an instant messenger list: **78%**

People in a social network community: **86%**

Source: Circuits of Cool/Digital Playground, July 2007

In order to engage with how media products are made, you could try the activities below.

• Explore the CNN Newsroom web site to find out the latest news and read behind the scenes stories. http://www.cnn.com/

• Find out which media giant makes a media product that you own or want to buy. In which country is the company based? Can you find out more about its global connections?

• Choose someone you know who has a cell phone and find out how long they've had it, how long they might keep it, and how many different cells they've had. What will they do with the phone when they finish with it? Use the internet to investigate the options.

Key Terms for Internet Searches

Type these terms into a search engine on the internet and see what results you get. How many hits appear? Are the web sites from around the world, and are there any information sources that surprise you?

- Advertising standards
- Censorship China
- Citizen media
- Data protection
- Digital divide
- Electronic waste (or e-waste)
- Global media industry

- Illegal downloads
- Media regulation
- Media takeover
- Press freedom
- User-generated content
- Web 2.0

Further Information and Web Sites

Books

Accept No Substitutes: The History of American Advertising
by Christina Mierau
(Lerner Publishing Group, 2000)

Brand Child
by Martin Lindstrom and Patricia B Seybold
(Kogan Press, 2004)

Introduction To Mass Communication: Media Literacy and Culture
by Stanley J Baran
(McGraw-Hill, 2005)

Web Sites

Due to the changing nature of Internet links, Rosen Publishing has developed an online list of Web sites related to the subject of this book. This site is updated regularly. Please use this link to access this list:
http://www.rosenlinks.com/glin/media

Topic Web

Use this topic web to discover the themes and ideas in subject areas related to the media and communications industry.

Geography
1. Mark on a map where your phone and computer were made, and where the music you like listening to comes from. How global are you?
2. Choose a country that you do not know much about. Investigate the country through each of the subindustries in this book—by reading a news story about it, by looking at some of its ads, by listening to a musician from that country, and by reading some blogs written by citizens of that country.

Citizenship
1. Choose an issue in this book that is important to you, such as music sharing or media control. How can you publicize your opinions and achieve what you want? You could hold a class debate.
2. Imagine you are the editor for a global news network. Decide which stories are most important to broadcast and why, from: a) bad weather causing crops to fail in Mali b) another tanker has been seized off Somalia c) U.S. police conduct terrorist investigation d) Madonna plans a party for her children.

English
1. Use the web site http://www.world-newspapers.com to select any three news sites from countries around the world. Do they have any similar headlines? Is the style of writing the same on all three sites?
2. Write an article for a news web site describing how much young people use the media in all its different formats.

The Media and Communications Industry

Math
1. The average American encounters between 600 and 625 ads a day. Record how many ads you see in one day, in all the different formats, and calculate how many that is for a week and a year.

Science
1. Find out what the mineral inside cell phones, columbite tantalite, looks like, and how to get it out of the ground.
2. List the different formats available for storing music over the years (e.g. cassette tape, CD). Discuss the pros and cons of each storage method.

IT
1. Investigate the different web addresses .gov, .org, .com, .edu, .co.uk, and .tv mean. Are there any that you would trust more? Why?
2. Media literacy is about knowing which information, facts, and web sites to trust. Consider a web site you use often; where does the information come from and how is it presented?

Glossary

asset something owned by a company that makes the company valuable, such as financial assets (e.g. investments) and fixed assets (e.g. buildings).

blog a web log on a web site that has regular entries, with comments, opinions, and sometimes recommendations, images, and videos.

brand a symbol, mark, or quality that characterizes a product.

citizen media describes the way that audiences can now participate in news media, even if they are not journalists.

conglomerate a corporation made up of several different businesses, sometimes in different industries.

consolidate when businesses consolidate, they merge, or are taken over, to make one conglomerate.

cookies packets of data that are sent from a web server to a web client, and can be used to keep information about web users, such as their buying preferences.

copyright a form of intellectual property that gives the creator of an original work (e.g. a song) control over how that work is published and distributed.

digital communication the electronic transmission of information that has been encoded digitally, for processing or storage on computers.

diversification establishing new products and markets, sometimes outside normal areas of business, to increase sales

diversify to create different forms, so digital communication has allowed news products to diversify into articles, web pages, video, and newspapers.

greenhouse gases atmospheric gases, such as carbon dioxide, methane, nitrous oxide, and water vapor, that contribute to the greenhouse effect that is warming the planet.

interdependent when organizations, industries, or individuals are mutually dependent on each other to make something work.

less developed countries (LDCs) countries that have a lower income and poorer standards in health, nutrition, education, and industry than more developed countries (MDCs).

merchandise the range of goods available for sale.

merger the combining of two or more companies.

more developed countries (MDCs) countries that have a higher income and better standards in health, nutrition, education, and industry than less developed countries (LDCs).

multimedia media and content that is available in different forms such as print, video, etc.

neutrality the position of being neutral, without any bias or leaning toward a particular side or viewpoint.

oligopoly the market condition that exists when there are only a few sellers who each have a large market share.

outsource to subcontract work to other economies, often elsewhere in the world, where production is cheaper.

podcast an audio broadcast that has been converted into an audio file for playback on a media device, such as a phone or an mp3 player.

subindustry one specialized industry within a wider industry.

sustainable able to be maintained at a steady level for a long time, without causing environmental or social damage.

transnational company (TNC) a company that operates across several nations.

United Nations Educational, Scientific and Cultural Organization (UNESCO) an organization that works to raise public awareness about the best use of communication resources (among other things).

United Nations (UN) a group of 192 member states that works globally in many areas, including peace, international law, health, education, and human rights.

user-generated content any content that is generated by users online, such as web-clicks, the terms entered into search engines, blogs, or messages.

World Trade Organization (WTO) An organization that deals with global rules of trade.

Index